ISBN-13: 0-9745660-4-7

Production by Farid Tabaian, Singletrack Maps www.singletrackmapping.com

Disclaimer
Mountain biking and training for mountain biking are potentially dangerous. Race Line Publishing, the author and their representatives assume no liability whatsoever for any damages associated in any way with the information contained herein.
Before you start any workout program, check with your physician. If you have any questions or concerns, consult a qualified trainer near you.

Props
Lester Pardoe, Coaching Specialist at the Boulder Center for Sports Medicine. Lester got me started on building my base, and he inspired me to embrace pedaling as a skill. I learned a lot in his PowerMax classes and with the Center's SpinScan system.

Neal Henderson, MS, CSCS, Elite & Olympic Cycling Coach at the Boulder Center for Sports Medicine. His "Winter Cycling Training" lecture lays out a proven approach much like this one. The weekly interval progression is adapted from Henderson's lecture.
www.bouldersportsmedicine.org

Cover photo by VAST::www.vastaction.com

This book and program are dedicated to my three-year-old twin girls Finley and Fiona, and to my wife Arlette, who wrangled them while I worked on this.

Finley and Fiona work their climbing skills at Valmont Bike Park in Boulder, CO.

CONTENTS

As mountain bikers, we pedal a lot. The smoother The smoother and more powerfully you can pedal, the better. Jim Norman and Tony Santoro earn turns in Lake Tahoe, CA and Bootleg Canyon, NV.

WHY ARE WE DOING THIS?

Mountain biking is awesome, and the better you are, the better it gets. We basically have two ways to improve our performance (and fun) on the bike:

Rocking the rocks: Some smart trainer time will help give you the skills and fitness to pedal right up the trickiest sections. Photo by Yosei Ikeda.

Improved skills. See the books Mastering Mountain Bike Skills, Teaching Mountain Bike Skills, Pro BMX Skills and Welcome to Pump Track Nation or take a clinic with me.

Improved fitness. Mountain bike fitness encompasses lots of different areas, including:

- Stability
- Agility
- Strength
- Power (these top four items should be developed off the bike)
- Long-term capacity and endurance (how fast can you ride for an hour?)
- Short-term capacity and endurance (how fast can you ride for a few minutes?)
- Fully pinned power (how fast can you ride for a few seconds?)

While you should work on your riding skills and off-bike physical abilities, pedaling is our bread and butter. It's how we get around, and the cardiovascular benefits translate to other aspects of our riding game (pumping terrain for example).

This program focuses on pedaling power and overall workload tolerance. Specifically, it will help you sustain higher power for longer periods, and it will teach you to reach higher highs.

The third way to improve is confidence. That comes from successfully using your improved skills and fitness on sweet terrain.

What's different about this approach?

This program aims to help you develop cycling power AND skills in a way that most programs do not address. You are not just a hamster in a wheel. You are a Rider – an athlete – and I want every minute you spend on the trainer to help you rip.

Rather than merely tell you to maintain a certain effort level for a certain amount of time (that's been done plenty), this program integrates both physical work and skill development. In one to three hours per week, you will dramatically increase your ability to have fun on the bike.

THE MISSION

Pump Up the Base is a simple, effective program for winter ("off season") bike training.

Winter and early spring are a perfect time to rock this adventure. Ideally, you'll Pump Up the Base two days per week, work off-bike stability/agility/strength/power two days a week and otherwise do fun stuff and recover. When you finish this program you'll be ready to wax your buddies or start higher-intensity interval work and crush the races. Either way, you'll be stronger and faster than before.

When you finish Pump Up the Base, check out Prepare to Pin It at leelikesbikes.com.

The Prepare to Pin It in-season training system will get you into awesome all-around riding shape.

More specifically, when you Pump Up the Base you will:

- Build aerobic capacity, neuromuscular power and neuromuscular coordination

- Be able to ride harder, longer

- Learn to pedal more smoothly and powerfully both in and out of the saddle

- Increase your top cadence

- Increase your peak power

- Broaden your powerband

- Stress your body enough to make you improve, but not beat you down

- Use your time very efficiently

- Not go as insane this winter

Wintertime trainer and pump track intervals will make you a monster in spring. Lee in his backyard dojo.

These workouts are fun and effective any time of year, but winter is a great time to build your aerobic engine and develop new pedaling skills.

www.leelikesbikes.com

WHAT YOU'LL BE DOING

In this program, you will focus on two specific intensity levels:

Sweet spot: Medium-hard for minutes

Pinned: As hard as you can for seconds

While you bang out the work, you'll also be practicing pedaling drills, refining your seated stroke, gaining efficiency out of the saddle and practicing your sit-stand transitions.

I suppose you'll need a warmup and rest periods too.

If you're pushing above your comfort zone but not into all-out discomfort, you're right around the sweet spot.

Sweet spot training

Why are we doing this?

- You will be able to maintain more power/work when you ride.

- You will be able to recover more quickly from hard efforts.

- Sustainable power is the bread and butter of a cyclist. It's literally what gets you around on the bike.

What is the sweet spot?

This is the intensity zone that gives you the best balance of physiological stress, duration, repeatability and adaptation. In short, you get the most bang for your buck – without beating yourself down so much you don't finish the program.

Put even more simply: Pedaling in the sweet spot gives you the greatest increase in your sustained power with the least amount of fatigue. Less fatigue means you can finish your workouts and finish this program.

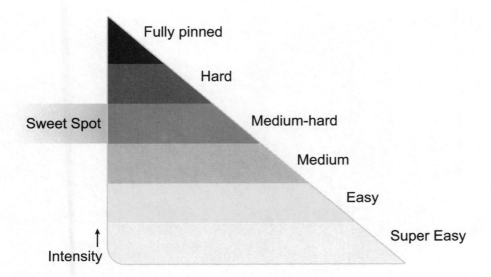

How do you know you're in the sweet spot?

The sweet spot is medium-hard (or orange-red). You're not cruising (that's lower-level aerobic base), and you're not pinning it (that's higher-level anaerobic work). Sweet spot intensity takes some focus to maintain. It's not crazy difficult, but you do have to pay attention.

- If you have a power meter, sweet spot is around 85-100% of your threshold power. Threshold power is roughly your average power over a 20-minute time trial. Try one and see where you are.

- If you have a heart rate monitor, it's around 75-85% of your max heart rate.

- If you have lungs and a voice box, it's as hard as you can go while speaking. If you can say the entire Pledge of Allegiance, you're at the low end. If you can speak only in short sentences, you're at the high end. If you can't talk, you're going too hard.

> If you can maintain 90-100% of your threshold power, you'll get more bang for your buck.

What if you are tired?

If you are tired, work the easier end of the range. If you feel great, work the higher end of the range. But don't go above the sweet spot; save your energy for awesome sprints.

How long do I have to stay in the sweet spot?

We'll start with three-minute intervals. This doesn't sound like a challenge, but it will not be easy.

By the end of this program, you'll be able to hold sweet-spot power for 20 minutes several times in a workout (with some sprints and drills thrown in because we are Riders, not riders).

Sprinting – fully pinned

Fully pinned at full extension. The more you sprint like an elite BMXer, the better. Coach Greg Romero gets some at the Olympic Training Center in Chula Vista, CA. From the book Pro BMX Skills.

Why are we doing this?

- Increase your max pedaling cadence.
- Increase your max power.

In the real world, this will translate to a quicker, smoother pedal stroke and more power on tap when you need it.

What is fully pinned?

Exercise physiologists refer to this intensity level as neuromuscular power.

Neuromuscular power has nothing to do with aerobic or endurance fitness. It's more like the power you see on weight lifters and dirt jumpers. How fast can your legs move? How much freaking power can you produce, even for just a moment?

Why does this matter?

The faster and more powerfully you can pedal, the more oomph you have when you need it and the easier it is to pedal at lower intensities.

As my high school strength coach used to say, in long socks and short shorts, "Anything a weak muscle can do, a strong muscle can do better."

What does that mean to me?

When it's time to sprint, you are going to pin it. Full gas – all or nothing – until you peak. Five, 10, maybe 15 seconds. That's it. We want high rpm and huge wattage.

As a matter of fact, please get better at reaching your peak power sooner. An elite BMXer can hit peak power (over 1,500 watts) between a dead stop and the fifth stroke. Bam!

You're already working the sweet spot at 200-something watts. I don't care how long you can maintain 500 watts. I want to see you bust out 1,000 watts, then sit down and maintain 200.

When will I be sprinting?

This program has two workouts for each week: A and B. During workout A, you will sprint at the indicated peaks.

At the beginning of this program, you'll be sprinting at the beginning of each interval.

As you gain fitness and ferocity — and intervals become 10 minutes and longer — we'll be adding sprints within your intervals. If you have the energy, you'll be sprinting every five minutes or so. If you are tired, skip a sprint (there's no sense practicing slowness and weakness).

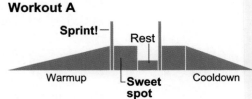

Workout A

Again, the sprints are about quality. Spin as fast as you freaking can. As soon as your speed starts to crumble, sit down and try to maintain sweet spot power.

How do I sprint?

If your sprint is at the beginning of an interval, start from a dead stop or very low rpm, then pin it. Use an easy gear that you can move quickly. Leg speed is the goal. Focus on violent downstrokes. As elite BMX coach Greg Romero says: "Bam! Bam! Bam!"

If your sprint is during an interval, jump from sweet spot cadence/power to full gas as fast as you can. Imagine a sprint finish or a technical power move. If you can wind your sweet spot gear from 80 to 200 rpm, that would be great. If you need to shift to an easier gear, that's fine.

What about recovery?

In this program, after you sprint you don't get to spin easy and look online for cool truck rims. We are mountain bikers, and sprinting is an integral part of our flow.

After you sprint, settle in and try to maintain sweet spot power. If you sprint correctly (FULL GAS!) you'll have to drop below the sweet spot to recover. Strive to regain sweet spot power as soon as you can. Anyone who climbs rock gardens will know how this applies to the real world.

What's the point again?

These sprints will develop your muscles and the electrical system that fires them. As a skills instructor, I see many high-level riders who have no idea how powerful they can be … because they never find out.

We're gonna find out this winter. Then we're gonna make you even more powerful.

> On my LeMond Revolution, I like to start in the 34x17 (210 rpm and 1,500 watts so far) then shift to the 50 and settle in (~100 rpm and 250 watts).

Warmup

You can get a nice warmup in 15 minutes:

- 10 minutes – Start easy and work your way up to sweet spot power. You should be sweating and breathing like you're on a bike ride.

- 4 minutes – 15-second bursts with 45 seconds easy spinning

- 1 minute – Get off the bike and stretch whatever is tight. Take as much time as you need.

- OK, now pin it.

I don't advise this, but if I'm busy I use my first interval as my warmup. I just start easy and ease my way up to speed.

If I'm really busy — if I only have 10 minutes to ride — I sit down and hammer at the top of the sweet spot. I cool down by going back to work or playing with my girls.

Rest

Between each interval you will enjoy a rest period. What you do with that time is up to you. Some ideas:

- Spin very easily. Stand up and stretch on the bike.

- Sit down and maintain yellow intensity. If you feel good enough to ride orange, you need to work harder when it's time to work.

- Spin easy to get the heart rate down then get off the bike. Depending on how I feel, I either stretch what's tight or do some mobility/strength work.

The main goal: Recover so you execute the next interval with perfect form and Strava KOM power.

A productive way to spend a minute.

Cooldown

The goal is to get back to normal heart rate and laziness without shocking your body.

Ideally:

- Spin easily and long enough to get your heart rate down to 100 or so. You should not be breathing hard. Depending on your intensity and fitness, this might take 5 or 10 minutes.

- Stretch whatever's tight. Do some light mobility/ strength work.

Clean up your sweat!

HOW DOES THIS FIT INTO THE REST OF MY PROGRAM?

Your complete training program goes beyond the scope of this work, but here are some ideas for your winter:

- Strive to rock this program at least once a week, preferably twice. One trainer session and one session on a real bike (or on the pump track!) would be good.

- Mix in some lower-intensity base work. At this intensity you can hold a conversation. If you have time, go for long, sweet rides. But this does not have to be on a bike: go hiking or cross-country skiing. Ride moto. If you don't have lots of time, do physical stuff whenever you can: Jog places. Shovel your driveway. Build a pump track.

- Develop your off-bike stability, agility, strength and power. You can do this work in the gym, your garage or around your neighborhood. Professional Xterra racer and endurance coach Cody Waite says strength is the first link in your performance chain.

- Do what works for you. A good program is tailored to you. If you're tired, rest. If you feel great, pin it. When in question, ask a qualified trainer.

- Have fun!

Man doesn't live on a trainer alone. Go out and ride! You'll feel stronger after only a few weeks of this program. Photo by Yosei Ikeda.

STUFF YOU NEED

Need is a strong word. How about must-haves and nice-to-haves?

Must have

Some kind of stationary bike setup. The ones at the gym are OK, but your own real bike on a trainer is best.

This program is designed for stationary trainers, but you can do the same work outside. Outside is more gratifying. Inside is easier to measure (and more doable for busy people in cold places).

A stopwatch, clock or other timing device.

Hey, use what you've got.

Nice to have

Power meter

The best and only real way to measure power. On-bike power meters work everywhere (except the pump track). The best trainers have integrated power meters, and they don't have to be expensive.

Speedometer

If you don't have a power meter, wheel speed is an acceptable way to measure relative work.

The LeMond Power Pilot computer counts revolutions so you can just pin it.

Heart rate monitor

This is your body's tachometer. It's fun to correlate your heart rate with power. If you don't have a way to measure power or speed, you can work based on heart rate.

Cadence meter

These are awesome. If your bike or trainer doesn't have one, you can count strokes for 15, 20, 30 or 60 seconds then do the math. This will keep you busy, but it'll be hard to find your absolute max cadence.

A really nice trainer

Whichever trainer you have is fine. Ride the darn thing. If you're looking for a trainer, consider:

- Magnetic or fluid resistance is good for all-around training.

- Wind resistance is loud.

- Rollers are great for skill, according to traditional wisdom, but you have to be very skilled to freaking pin it. I prefer to be attached to the trainer, so I'm not worrying about crashing.

- If you're a powerful rider, check the max resistance of your trainer.

I use a LeMond Revolution trainer, which is the Shimano XTR of indoor trainers:

- The bike's chain mounts to a cassette on the trainer, so there's no wheel slip.

- The heavy flywheel simulates acceleration.

- The big fan generates lots of top-end resistance (but it's loud).

- The integrated Power Pilot computer tracks power, cadence and heart rate.

- This thing is sturdy and stable.

Hydration

At least one 16-ounce bottle per workout.

Ventilation

You will get hot. Crack the window. Run a fan.

Hygiene

Clean up your sweat before your wife notices the odor.

LeMond Revolution Trainer

My office setup.

Let's talk pedals

Flat and clip-in pedals.

Most of you ride and/or race in clip-in pedals, and that's fine. I encourage you all to rock this program (or at least parts of it) with flat pedals. Here's why:

- Real skill. With nothing to hold your feet on the pedals, you will learn to push in the direction the pedal is going. You will learn the circle in a whole new, more integrated way. You will learn to *pedal* in circles, rather than get your feet dragged in circles.

- Freedom. You won't feel so locked to the bike ... because ... you're not.

- Convenience. No time to change shoes? Just hop on and pedal! My trainer is in my office, and I often hop on for a 10-minute de-stresser.

- Perfect foot placement. Ideally, your foot will be in the same place in relation to your pedal spindle no matter which style pedal you use. After some time to learn the flats, check out where your feet end up. Without the clips to limit your movement, your feet will find the perfect spot on the pedal. Should you change your cleat placement?

If you like to ride/race clipped in, be sure to rock your clips toward the end of this program. We want your skills to translate to the real world. Chances are if you learn to pedal well with flats, you'll be even better clipped in.

Braaap!

> Two elite racers I convinced to rock flats for the winter have reported eight percent increases in power – at the same heart rate — this spring compared to last spring.

> Flats teach you how to pedal, and they can add confidence in sketchy situations. First descent on North Red Trail near Boulder, CO

> When I switched from flats back to clips in Spring 2012, I instantly found 20 more peak rpm and 250 more peak watts, and I improved my sustained climbing significantly.

HOW TO PEDAL

Pedaling is a skill like any other, and given the number of revolutions we crank out over the years, it makes sense to get great at pedaling.

When I say great, I mean efficient, comfortable and as powerful as you can be. Even if you weren't born with a climber's body — and even if you were — you can always learn to be more efficient, comfortable and powerful.

Our goal

The muscles that push out-power the muscles that pull. We will not focus on pulling back or up on the recovery stroke. Instead, we will focus on making the power stroke as long and powerful as possible. Our method? Just as we learn to move our feet with varying terrain, we will learn to move our feet with the arc of the pedals.

Pay attention to posture

You probably sit wrong all day at work. Get lazy and weak all you want when you're with the civilians. This program is all about quality, so pay attention:

No slumping on the bars. Ideally, your hands are weightless. A little pressure down and back is fine. Never – ever! – collapse forward. If you're that tired, get off your bike and do 100 burpees. Those are for punishment.

Engaged core. Again, no slumping! Do you know your tranversus abdominus? Maybe not. It's like a girdle that surrounds your midsection and ties your ribs to your hips. While you are pedaling, try to engage that muscle. Pull your belly button in and up. Pull the sides of your belly inward. The more stable your core, the more power you have, and the less your back is likely to hurt.

Hips and spine together. Don't be sitting with your hips in barstool position (straight up) then bending your back to reach your bars. Keep your hips and spine aligned with each other. Strive for a firm, yet relaxed curve in your back. If you don't know what I'm talking about, take a yoga class. Yogis are all about posture.

Basic seated pedaling

This is the bread and butter of cycling. The better you get at pedaling in the saddle, the more fun you're gonna have.

On steep climbs you have to bring your shoulders forward to maintain balance. Otherwise try to relax and keep your hips and spine in line. Photo by Yosei Ikeda.

When you pedal, consider two coinciding cycles:

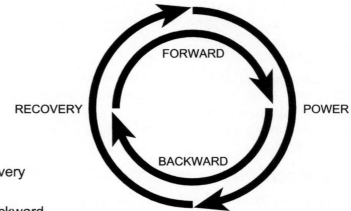

1. Power and recovery

2. Forward and backward

The actual angles vary depending on body position, terrain and pedaling style, but it's simple to think about these cycles in terms of a clock: 12, 3, 6 and 9 o'clock.

Power and recovery

You know about this one.

Power

Everyone who's ridden a bike is familiar with the power phase. If you want to move forward, you push the pedal down.

Recovery

While one pedal is being powered downward, the other is recovering upward.

Many of you have been told to pull up, but studies show pulling doesn't do much good unless you are in a very high torque, low rpm situation like a gate start or getting caught in a too-high gear. You'll enjoy the greatest benefit by making your power phase as long and strong as possible.

Now things get interesting:

Forward-backward

Forward-backward is an evolution of the technique of "ankling," in which you drop your heel at the top of the stroke and point your toes at the bottom. Thanks to Lester Pardoe at the Boulder Center for Sports Medicine for starting me on the ankling path.

Foot/pedal angles
In the saddle
90 rpm, cruising at 250 watts

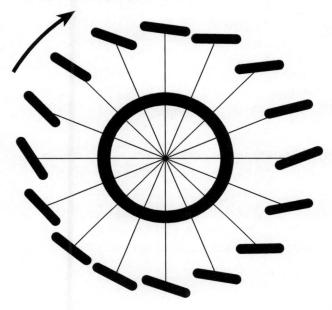

Forward

If your pedal is moving forward, try to get your foot behind it so you can push forward.

As your pedal starts moving forward past about 9 o'clock, start dropping your heel. This gives your power phase an early, smooth beginning. In other words, it helps you push sooner.

Try to start pushing forward before 12 o'clock.

Your heel will be lowest at about 3 o'clock.

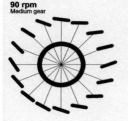
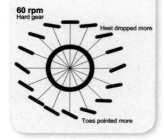
Backward

If your pedal is moving backward, try to get your foot in front of it so you can pull back. Even if you're not pulling very hard compared with the opposite push, try to be engaged with the backward motion.

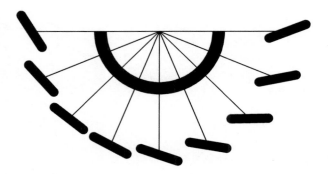

As your pedal starts moving backward past about 3 o'clock, start pointing your toes. This gives your power phase a later, smoother end. In other words, it helps you push longer.

Concentrate on pointing your toes between 3 and 6 o'clock. Your heel continues to rise from 6 to 9 o'clock, but that's a function of your knee bending. The main engagement happens between 3 and 6.

Your heel will be highest at about 9 o'clock.

Forward and backward at the same time

At first, focus on dropping your heel across the top. When that becomes semi-automatic, work on pointing your toes across the bottom. When you can do both drills decently, alternate 10 strokes of each. When that makes sense, it's time to put them together.

Pedaling is a cycle. Hmm, cycling? While one leg is powering, the other is recovering. While one foot is pushing forward, the other is pulling backward. When you're ready:

Work the opposition. While one heel is dropping, start pointing the opposite toes.

This is simple in theory, but – dude – it's hard in real life. This will keep your mind busy during those trainer sessions. As with any new skill, start at low speed (cadence) and work your way up.

You don't need to focus on the middle of the power phase; you already know how to mash down on the pedals. If you practice the beginning and end of your power phase (the top and bottom of your stroke), you will make your power stroke longer and more powerful.

Pedaling out of the saddle

A great mountain biker can maintain the same beautiful pedal stroke whether she's sitting, standing or anywhere in between. We'll explore the details in another book, but here are the keys.

Balance!

If you've read Mastering Mountain Bike Skills, Teaching Mountain Bike Skills or Pro BMX Skills, you know it's all about heavy feet and light hands.

When you get out of the saddle, keep your hands light!

When you stand up on steep dirt, does your rear wheel spin out? I'll bet yes. That's a sure sign you're collapsing onto your bars. Uncool. Weak. Ineffective!

When you get out of the saddle, keep your hands weightless. Make small balance corrections by moving your hips back and forth.

Sweep through the bottom.

Do not stand on your pedal at the bottom of the stroke, not even for an instant.

Instead, keep your pedal moving right through the bottom.

You can try the old scraping poo off your shoe trick, but you'll get more boost when you focus on dropping the opposite heel and pushing across the top of the stroke.

So freaking steep! Believe it or not, I honed this technique on the trainer. Photo by Farid Tabaian

Alignment

You've been doing the yoga and dead lifts, right?

Imagine carrying a heavy television. You wouldn't do that hunched over, would you? Heck no: you'd drive your hips forward, between your shoulders and feet, and support the weight with your skeleton.

It should be the same on a bike, especially if you're pushing a hard gear.

- When you stand up to pedal, drive your hips forward and extend your body upward (not forward onto the bars).
- Hands should stay light.
- Arms should be pretty straight (that's all about bike fit, another book, coming soon).

As this starts to make sense, practice clean transitions from sitting to standing and back. Strive for light hands and an unchanging spin.

Practice perfectly

Every time you pedal poorly, you get even better at … pedaling poorly.

As much as you can, embrace your trainer time as focused pedaling skill development.

Listen. Strive for a smoother, rounder sound.

Always be mindful of your posture.

Work the sitting heel drop, toe point then both. Do this at various cadences.

Strive for clean alignment, good balance and efficient pedal stroke out of the saddle. Yes, in all gears, at all rpms.

Good posture is good posture, whether you're at the grocery store or on your bike. Shoulder blades down and back, hips and spine in line. Photo by Yosei Ikeda.

As you practice the new skills, focus your mental effort on your "dumb" leg, which is usually your left. Your right leg will figure out what to do.

When you're working this program, never EVER just sit there and mash like an idiot. What a waste of time that would be. Focus on your cadence, your pedal stroke, great posture, something useful.

As you integrate these new pedaling skills, you will begin to transition seamlessly between power and recovery, forward and backward. By that time your pedal stroke will be round, smooth and very powerful. Braaap!

Expand your powerband

Powerband is a moto term, and we sure love to braaap, so we're all about the moto terms.

An engine's powerband is the rpm range where it makes the most useful power. An old four-stroke trail bike has a low powerband, like a tractor. A two-stroke motocrosser has a high powerband, like a hummingbird.

Most cyclists tend to work in a narrow range of rpm, say 50-75. That's fine if you're always in the perfect gear, and if you love shifting all the time, and if you're not in any particular hurry.

As kung fu pedaling masters, we are going to broaden our powerbands. Depending on the situation, you will be an XR650 trail bike, a CR125 motocross bike or something in between. Our goals for this program:

- Teach you to make usable power at lower rpm. From zero on up.

- Make your default spin faster. Go from, say, 70 rpm to 90 rpm. Studies show that a faster default spin will help you climb longer, faster and more efficiently. Why? It shifts work from your muscles to your cardiovascular system.

- Learn to make effective power at even higher rpm. Be able to crank, say, 120 rpm when you need it. A short, steep climb is a great example. Another is powering out of a tight corner.

- Make your peak rpm as high as possible.

To help you accomplish these goals, you'll be doing intervals at various speeds.

In the program, I'll ask you to pedal at these speeds.

Mountain biker powerbands

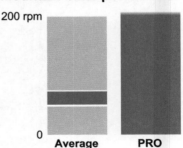

> **60 rpm.** Get into a hard gear. It should feel like climbing a steep hill. Fast enough to turn the pedals over, but slow enough that you have to find muscles to do the work. On some trainers you won't get enough resistance. Do your best.
>
> **90 rpm.** This will be your new default. If you can only do 80, that's fine but work your way to 90. If 90 is easy, work your way up to 100.
>
> **120 rpm.** As fast as you can spin for 30 seconds. 120 rpm is a fine goal. Work your way up to it — then beyond.
>
> **Sprint.** Fully pinned. No pacing. No apologies. Turn it to 11. When you reach 200 rpm, you're getting somewhere. An elite BMXer can spin over 250.

Pick a gear or trainer resistance that lets you maintain the indicated workload while pushing the called-for rpm.

Here are my gears this season on a LeMond Revolution trainer, Specialized S-Works Tricross, Shimano Ultegra SL compact road gearing:

Sweet spot power

60-70 rpm – 50x11

90-100 rpm – 50x17

120-150 rpm – 50x21

Pinned

From a stop - 34x17* – max rpm (about 210 rpm right now**)

In the middle of an interval – 50x17 – max power (about 1,500 watts right now**)

*The same gear-inches as a BMX bike.

**I expect more after this winter!

Road and cyclocross bikes have the most usable gearing for indoor trainer sessions. My Specialized S-Works Tricross has a Shimano Ultegra SL drivetrain with 50/34 chainrings and an 11-28 cassette.

HOW TO FOLLOW THIS PROGRAM

Discipline

Follow this program precisely.

Or don't.

This program is a suggestion. A template. If you can follow it exactly, good for you. But:

- If you're tired, take it easy. Do fewer intervals. Skip some sprints. Maintain lower sweet spot power.

- If you feel strong, ride higher in the sweet spot or or add some sprints.

If you get to week nine (or five or 10 or whenever) and decide you don't want to do even longer/harder trainer workouts, I understand. Here are some options:

- Repeat that workout while improving your technique and power,

- Go outside and ride for real, or

- Start higher-intensity intervals and go crush some races.

Consistency!

Whatever you do, be consistent week to week. If you only have time for part of the workout, do as much as you can with great form and high intensity.

Neal Henderson at the Boulder Center for Sports Medicine says aerobic fitness takes 5-10 years of consistent work to fully develop. Be consistent week to week and season to season.

Over the past three winters, I've seen noticeable jumps in my sweet zone power, max cadence and max power. Because of my quality workouts, I'm out-climbing riders who used to crush me — while I'm entering my mid-40s and riding less than ever.

Stay in the sweet spot

Remember, we are not trying to beat you down — especially in December.

If you get into the red zone (very possible after a sprint or standing interval!) back off. Sit and turn an easy gear until you reach the orange zone, then get back to the sweet spot.

This program only works if you can do the workout and keep it up for 12 (or nine) weeks.

Consistency. Ride medium-hard now so you can ride hard next summer.

Do I really have to ride a trainer?

Indoor trainers provide the easiest consistency and measurement. That's why fitness professionals love them.

If you want to do this work outside, go for it.

Road bikes with power meters are used by many top mountain bikers. You get a precise workout, and you get to be outside.

Mountain bikes on trail are way more fun, but less precise time- and effort-wise. Use climbs for intervals and descents for recovery. Yeah, that actually sounds ideal!

If you have the skill and strength to ride pump track in the sweet spot, a pump track is a great place for some of your workouts. When it's time to sprint, do one lap as fast as you can. Otherwise, try to maintain orange-red effort.

Most humans jump straight into the red zone on pump tracks. Until you are super dialed, pump-tracking is anaerobic. When you can rip laps aerobically (for 10, 20 minutes or longer), that's a sure sign of kung fu.

A pump track is an awesome place for intervals. By lap 87 you'll find some smoothness for sure. Photo by Heather Irmiger

Lee McCormack on Stumpy 29
www.leelikesbikes.com

The longer the workouts get, the more you'll want to do them outside. How about Workout A on the trainer and Workout B in the real world?

If you're outside, don't sweat the details. Do your best to follow the spirit of the workout. Even better, adapt it to your terrain and needs.

Sitting vs. standing

Some intervals are marked as sitting. Get cozy and grind out the power.

Some intervals call for standing. If you can stand for the prescribed amount of time, that's impressive but not expected. Stand as long as you can with good form. When you can't stand standing, transition back to the saddle. When you feel better, try to stand again. Heck, the up/down/up transition is great practice.

Sprinting

When you sprint, get out of the saddle and punch it. Crush that downstroke! As you get on top of the gear, settle onto the nose of the saddle and try to find even more speed.

When the rpm/power start to drop, back off.

Not 8 or 9 or even 10.

11!

THE INTERVALS

The core of this program is a series of ever-longer work periods. Nerds call these "intervals."

Here is the interval progression:

Week	Number of intervals	Minutes on	Minutes off	Minutes of work	Workout minutes*
1	6	3	2	18	30
2	5	4	3	20	35
3	5	5	3	25	40
4	5	6	3	30	45
5	4	8	4	32	48
6	3	10	3	30	39
7	4	10	3	40	52
8	3	15	5	45	60
9	2	20	5	40	50
10	3	17	5	51	66
11	4	15	5	60	80
12	3	20	10	60	90

*Not including recommended 15-minute warmup and 10-minute cooldown.

Weeks 10-12 are going to get interesting, and the workouts are going to get noticeably longer. If you're satisfied at week nine, feel free to repeat that workout with higher quality (or go outside and Ride).

Important! If all you can do is maintain sweet spot power during these intervals, with some sprints mixed in, you will gain noticeable strength on the bike. This is where most training programs end. But we're about turning it to 11, so …

MAKE IT REAL WITH FOCUSED DRILLS

If you can bang out 20 minutes of sweet spot power in the saddle, with sprints at 0, 5, 10 and 15 minutes, that is impressive – and you'll feel the benefit on trail.

But this isn't your typical roadie program. We're going to give each block of time a specific focus. Here's why:

- A sweet mountain bike ride is not static. You're going up, down and all around. Slow, medium and fast. Sitting, standing, sitting, standing.

- You'll develop much more realistic, usable pedaling power. Not to mention enhanced posture and balance, as well as general toughness.

- You will not get bored! You'll never be doing the same thing for more than five minutes. As you start incorporating the following drills, every minute will become an adventure: An adventure in awesomeness.

Quality! If you are tired, just practice sitting and spinning. Recover so you can rock the next Super D.

Below are the foci for each drill. Some drills have multiple difficulty levels. Start at Cat 3 and work your way up to Cat 1. Maintain great technique. Quality, quality, quality!

Sitting

Purpose: Get very good at making smooth power while seated. This is sort of the anti-drill. If you aren't busy sprinting or standing, you should be here. Focus on your pedaling skill.

Choose a gear that lets you maintain 90 rpm at sweet spot power. Rock it.

Climbing

Purpose: Build strength for bigger gears. Get you used to steep inclines. Start dialing in that standing stroke. Get you balanced and comfortable out of the saddle.

Choose a gear that lets you maintain 60 rpm at sweet spot power. Put your front wheel on some books. Each copy of Mastering Mountain Bike Skills or Pro BMX Skills adds about a 2% grade. Since the 2.4-mile climb to my house averages 10 percent, I'll sometimes use five books.

Here are three versions of the climbing drill. Start with Cat 3 and work your way up.

Cat 3

- One minute sitting
- One minute standing
- One minute sitting
- One minute standing
- One minute sitting

Cat 2

- Two minutes standing
- One minute sitting
- Two minutes standing

Cat 1

- Five minutes standing

This is really hard … until you find your balance. Then you can sit or stand whenever you feel like it.

One key to technical climbing is smooth, balanced sit-stand transitions. Photo by Yosei Ikeda.

Ladder

Purpose: Smoothen your sit/stand/sit transitions. Maintain the same balance/effort/speed/power while sitting and standing. This skill forms the foundation of your technical climbing ability.

Strive for 90 rpm in and out of the saddle. If you need to upshift when you stand, that's normal, but work toward maintaining the same cadence in every position.

- 10 seconds standing/50 seconds sitting
- 20/40
- 30/30
- 40/20
- 50/10

Super D

Purpose: Be able to fully pin a pedally downhill. Learn to spike your pedal speed without spiking your effort level.

Maintain sweet spot power at both cadences. 90 rpm in sweet spot gear. 120 rpm in a lighter gear. (When the season nears, you'll do these intervals in the sweet spot gear).

Cat 3

120 rpm 10 seconds/90 rpm 50 seconds

Cat 2

120 rpm 20 seconds/90 rpm 40 seconds

Cat 1

120 rpm 30 seconds/90 rpm 30 seconds

Mixmaster

Purpose: Give you the widest powerband ever. Keep you focused during long intervals.

- Hard gear at 60 rpm for 20 seconds
- Normal gear at 90 rpm for 20 seconds
- Easy gear at 120 rpm for 20 seconds

Repeat for five minutes.

If you are too tired to execute these drills with beautiful form, back off. Spend more time in the saddle, skip a burst or whatever.

Remember: Merely maintaining 90 rpm and sweet spot power, with some sprints mixed in, is excellent for your mountain biking ability. The drills are bonus.

TWO WORKOUTS IN ONE

Ideally, you'll rock this program twice a week. One day you'll do Workout A, the other you'll do Workout B.

> "Train your weaknesses. Race your strengths."
> – Lester Pardoe

Workout A

Sprint when you see a peak. Then sit down and maintain sweet spot power.

Workout B

Ignore the peaks. Do the drills as indicated with these letters.

S – Sit. Normal gear.

C – Climb. Hard gear. Alternate sitting and standing.

L – Ladder. Normal gear. Alternate sitting and standing, with more and more time standing.

SD – Super D. Spin 120 rpm in easy gear. Turn 90 in normal gear. Repeat.

M – Mixmaster. Sitting. 20 seconds low cadence, 20 seconds medium cadence, 20 seconds high cadence.

Rest: Give yourself a few days of recovery between these workouts. Monday and Thursday are good trainer days because you can have a big adventure on Saturday and take care of chores on Sunday.

Choose: If you can only do one workout per week, do your least favorite. That's the one you need help with! Really. Or alternate workouts week to week. Or do some intervals with sprints and some with drills. Mix it up however you like (or, better, how you hate).

When you finish Pump Up the Base

You will have solid base fitness, plus higher top-end speed. What next?

Option 1:

Go out and ride (faster and easier than ever)! Pretty sweet.

Option 2:

To attain and maintain peak in-season fitness with minimal training time and stress, check out the Prepare to Pin It training system at www.leelikesbikes.com.

For Prepare to Pin It, Lee partnered with Coach Lester Pardoe at the Boulder Center for Sports Medicine. Now you can train with the same methods used to train all levels of riders — including the elite of the elite. This stuff works!

PREPARE TO PIN IT

A smart approach to mountain bike fitness

Perfect for
• Trail riders
• XC and endurance racers
• Enduro and downhill racers
• Everyone who wants to minimize training time and maximize fun
Including: The one bike workout all MTBers should do!

LEE McCORMACK

Author of Mastering Mountain Bike Skills, Teaching Mountain Bike Skills, Pro BMX Skills, Welcome to Pump Track Nation and Pump Up the Base

With Lester Pardoe, Coaching Specialist, Boulder Center for Sports Medicine

LEE
LIKES
BIKES

THE PROGRAM

The following page shows the actual protocols you'll be following.

The workout is shown as a gray shape, with the height of the shape correlating with your effort level.

Workout A

- Warm up.
- Whenever you see a peak, pin a sprint.
- Sit down and maintain sweet spot power for the rest of the interval.
- Rest in the low spots.
- Cool down.

Workout B

- Warm up.
- Ignore the peaks and sprints.
- Under each interval shape you will see letter icons. These tell you which skill drill to focus on (if you have the energy).

    S – Sit

    C – Climb

    L – Ladder

    SD – Super D

    M – Mixmaster

- Rest in the low spots.
- Cool down.

Have fun!

Pump Up The Base: weekly workouts

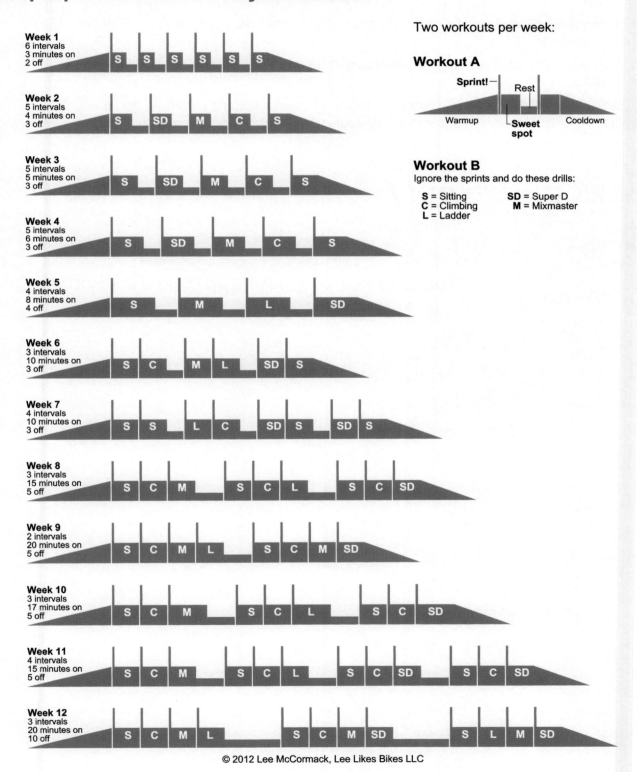

Week 1
6 intervals
3 minutes on
2 off

S S S S S S

Week 2
5 intervals
4 minutes on
3 off

S SD M C S

Week 3
5 intervals
5 minutes on
3 off

S SD M C S

Week 4
5 intervals
6 minutes on
3 off

S SD M C S

Week 5
4 intervals
8 minutes on
4 off

S M L SD

Week 6
3 intervals
10 minutes on
3 off

S C M L SD S

Week 7
4 intervals
10 minutes on
3 off

S S L C SD S SD S

Week 8
3 intervals
15 minutes on
5 off

S C M S C L S C SD

Week 9
2 intervals
20 minutes on
5 off

S C M L S C M SD

Week 10
3 intervals
17 minutes on
5 off

S C M S C L S C SD

Week 11
4 intervals
15 minutes on
5 off

S C M S C L S C SD S C SD

Week 12
3 intervals
20 minutes on
10 off

S C M L S C M SD S L M SD

Two workouts per week:

Workout A

Sprint! Rest

Warmup   Sweet spot   Cooldown

Workout B

Ignore the sprints and do these drills:

S = Sitting   **SD** = Super D
C = Climbing   **M** = Mixmaster
L = Ladder

WORKOUT DETAILS

Ideally, you'll do two Pump Up the Base workouts each week.

In Workout A you sprint for five seconds then sit at sweet spot power for the rest of the indicated work period.

In Workout B you do the indicated pedaling drills at sweet spot power for the indicated work period.

For an extra challenge, or if you can only do one of these workouts per week, go for Workout B — but sprint at the beginning of each pedaling drill. That's a real challenge!

WEEK 1 - WORKOUT A

Interval	Do this
Warmup	Build from Level 1 to sweet spot over 10-15min with some bursts mixed in
1	Sprint 5sec Sweet spot 2:55 Sitting Level 1 2min
3	Sprint 5sec Sweet spot 2:55 Sitting Level 1 2min
4	Sprint 5sec Sweet spot 2:55 Sitting Level 1 2min
5	Sprint 5sec Sweet spot 2:55 Sitting Level 1 2mins
6	Sprint 5sec Sweet spot 2:55 Sitting
Cooldown	Level 1 10-15min

WEEK 1 - WORKOUT B

Interval	Do this
Warmup	Build from Level 1 to sweet spot over 10-15min with some bursts mixed in
1	Sweet spot 3min Sitting Level 1 2min
3	Sweet spot 3min Sitting Level 1 2min
4	Sweet spot 3min Sitting Level 1 2min
5	Sweet spot 3min Sitting Level 1 2min
6	Sweet spot 3min Sitting Level 1 2min
Cooldown	Level 1 10-15min

WEEK 2 - WORKOUT A

Interval	Do this
Warmup	Build from Level 1 to sweet spot over 10-15min with some bursts mixed in
1	Sprint 5sec Sweet spot 3:55 Sitting Level 1 3min
2	Sprint 5sec Sweet spot 3:55 Sitting Level 1 3min
3	Sprint 5sec Sweet spot 3:55 Sitting Level 1 3min
4	Sprint 5sec Sweet spot 3:55 Sitting Level 1 3min
5	Sprint 5sec Sweet spot 2:55 Sitting
Cooldown	Level 1 10-15min

WEEK 2 - WORKOUT B

Interval	Do this
Warmup	Build from Level 1 to sweet spot over 10-15min with some bursts mixed in
1	Sweet spot 4min Sitting Level 1 3min
2	Sweet spot 4min Super D Level 1 3min
3	Sweet spot 4min Mixmaster Level 1 3min
4	Sweet spot 4min Climbing Level 1 3min
5	Sweet spot 4min Sitting
Cooldown	Level 1 10-15min

WEEK 3 - WORKOUT A

Interval	Do this
Warmup	Build from Level 1 to sweet spot over 10-15min with some bursts mixed in
1	Sprint 5sec Sweet spot 4:55 Sitting Level 1 3min
2	Sprint 5sec Sweet spot 4:55 Sitting Level 1 3min
3	Sprint 5sec Sweet spot 4:55 Sitting Level 1 3min
4	Sprint 5sec Sweet spot 4:55 Sitting Level 1 3min
5	Sprint 5sec Sweet spot 4:55 Sitting
Cooldown	Level 1 10-15min

WEEK 3 - WORKOUT B

Interval	Do this
Warmup	Build from Level 1 to sweet spot over 10-15min with some bursts mixed in
1	Sweet spot 5min Sitting Level 1 3min
2	Sweet spot 5min Super D Level 1 3min
3	Sweet spot 5min Mixmaster Level 1 3min
4	Sweet spot 5min Climbing Level 1 3min
5	Sweet spot 5min Sitting
Cooldown	Level 1 10-15min

WEEK 4 - WORKOUT A

Interval	Do this
Warmup	Build from Level 1 to sweet spot over 10-15min with some bursts mixed in
1	Sprint 5sec Sweet spot 5:55 Sitting Level 1 3min
2	Sprint 5sec Sweet spot 5:55 Sitting Level 1 3min
3	Sprint 5sec Sweet spot 5:55 Sitting Level 1 3min
4	Sprint 5sec Sweet spot 5:55 Sitting Level 1 3min
5	Sprint 5sec Sweet spot 5:55 Sitting
Cooldown	Level 1 10-15min

WEEK 4 - WORKOUT B

Interval	Do this
Warmup	Build from Level 1 to sweet spot over 10-15min with some bursts mixed in
1	Sweet spot 6min Sitting Level 1 3min
2	Sweet spot 6min Super D Level 1 3min
3	Sweet spot 6min Mixmaster Level 1 3min
4	Sweet spot 6min Climbing Level 1 3min
5	Sweet spot 6min Sitting
Cooldown	Level 1 10-15min

WEEK 5 - WORKOUT A

Interval	Do this
Warmup	Build from Level 1 to sweet spot over 10-15min with some bursts mixed in
1	Sprint 5sec Sweet spot 7:55 Sitting Level 1 4min
2	Sprint 5sec Sweet spot 7:55 Sitting Level 1 4min
3	Sprint 5sec Sweet spot 7:55 Sitting Level 1 4min
4	Sprint 5sec Sweet spot 7:55 Sitting
Cooldown	Level 1 10-15min

WEEK 5 - WORKOUT B

Interval	Do this
Warmup	Build from Level 1 to sweet spot over 10-15min with some bursts mixed in
1	Sweet spot 8min Sitting Level 1 4min
2	Sweet spot 8min Mixmaster Level 1 4min
3	Sweet spot 8min Ladder Level 1 4min
4	Sweet spot 8min Super D
Cooldown	Level 1 10-15min

WEEK 6 - WORKOUT A

Interval	Do this
Warmup	Build from Level 1 to sweet spot over 10-15min with some bursts mixed in
1	Sprint 5sec Sweet spot 4:55 Sitting Sprint 5sec Sweet spot 4:55 Sitting Level 1 3min
2	Sprint 5sec Sweet spot 4:55 Sitting Sprint 5sec Sweet spot 4:55 Sitting Level 1 3min
3	Sprint 5sec Sweet spot 4:55 Sitting Sprint 5sec Sweet spot 4:55 Sitting
Cooldown	Level 1 10-15min

WEEK 6 - WORKOUT B

Interval	Do this
Warmup	Build from Level 1 to sweet spot over 10-15min with some bursts mixed in
1	Sweet spot 5min Sitting Sweet spot 5min Climbing Level 1 3min
2	Sweet spot 5min Mixmaster Sweet spot 5min Ladder Level 1 3min
3	Sweet spot 5min Super D Sweet spot 5min Sitting
Cooldown	Level 1 10-15min

WEEK 7 - WORKOUT A

Interval	Do this
Warmup	Build from Level 1 to sweet spot over 10-15min with some bursts mixed in
1	Sprint 5sec Sweet spot 4:55 Sitting Sprint 5sec Sweet spot 4:55 Sitting Level 1 3min
2	Sprint 5sec Sweet spot 4:55 Sitting Sprint 5sec Sweet spot 4:55 Sitting Level 1 3min
3	Sprint 5sec Sweet spot 4:55 Sitting Sprint 5sec Sweet spot 4:55 Sitting Level 1 3min
4	Sprint 5sec Sweet spot 4:55 Sitting Sprint 5sec Sweet spot 4:55 Sitting
Cooldown	Level 1 10-15min

WEEK 7 - WORKOUT B

Interval	Do this
Warmup	Build from Level 1 to sweet spot over 10-15min with some bursts mixed in
1	Sweet spot 5min Sitting Sweet spot 5min Sitting Level 1 3min
2	Sweet spot 5min Ladder Sweet spot 5min Climbing Level 1 3min
3	Sweet spot 5min Super D Sweet spot 5min Sitting Level 1 3min
4	Sweet spot 5min Super D Sweet spot 5min Sitting
Cooldown	Level 1 10-15min

WEEK 8 - WORKOUT A

Interval	Do this
Warmup	Build from Level 1 to sweet spot over 10-15min with some bursts mixed in
1	Sprint 5sec Sweet spot 4:55 Sitting Sprint 5sec Sweet spot 4:55 Sitting Sprint 5sec Sweet spot 4:55 Sitting Level 1 5min
2	Sprint 5sec Sweet spot 4:55 Sitting Sprint 5sec Sweet spot 4:55 Sitting Sprint 5sec Sweet spot 4:55 Sitting Level 1 5min
3	Sprint 5sec Sweet spot 4:55 Sitting Sprint 5sec Sweet spot 4:55 Sitting Sprint 5sec Sweet spot 4:55 Sitting
Cooldown	Level 1 10-15min

WEEK 8 - WORKOUT B

Interval	Do this
Warmup	Build from Level 1 to sweet spot over 10-15min with some bursts mixed in
1	Sweet spot 5min Sitting Sweet spot 5min Climbing Sweet spot 5min Mixmaster Level 1 5min
2	Sweet spot 5min Sitting Sweet spot 5min Climbing Sweet spot 5min Ladder Level 1 5min
3	Sweet spot 5min Sitting Sweet spot 5min Climbing Sweet spot 5min Super D
Cooldown	Level 1 10-15min

WEEK 9 - WORKOUT A

Interval	Do this
Warmup	Build from Level 1 to sweet spot over 10-15min with some bursts mixed in
1	Sprint 5sec Sweet spot 4:55 Sitting Sprint 5sec Sweet spot 4:55 Sitting Sprint 5sec Sweet spot 4:55 Sitting Sprint 5sec Sweet spot 4:55 Sitting Level 1 5min
2	Sprint 5sec Sweet spot 4:55 Sitting Sprint 5sec Sweet spot 4:55 Sitting Sprint 5sec Sweet spot 4:55 Sitting Sprint 5sec Sweet spot 4:55 Sitting
Cooldown	Level 1 10-15min

WEEK 9 - WORKOUT B

Interval	Do this
Warmup	Build from Level 1 to sweet spot over 10-15min with some bursts mixed in
1	Sweet spot 5min Sitting Sweet spot 5min Climbing Sweet spot 5min Mixmaster Sweet spot 5min Ladder Level 1 5min
2	Sweet spot 5min Sitting Sweet spot 5min Climbing Sweet spot 5min Mixmaster Sweet spot 5min Super D
Cooldown	Level 1 10-15min

WEEK 10 - WORKOUT A

Interval	Do this
Warmup	Build from Level 1 to sweet spot over 10-15min with some bursts mixed in
1	Sprint 5sec Sweet spot 4:55 Sitting Sprint 5sec Sweet spot 4:55 Sitting Sprint 5sec Sweet spot 6:55 Sitting Level 1 5min
2	Sprint 5sec Sweet spot 4:55 Sitting Sprint 5sec Sweet spot 4:55 Sitting Sprint 5sec Sweet spot 6:55 Sitting Level 1 5min
3	Sprint 5sec Sweet spot 4:55 Sitting Sprint 5sec Sweet spot 4:55 Sitting Sprint 5sec Sweet spot 6:55 Sitting
Cooldown	Level 1 10-15min

WEEK 10 - WORKOUT B

Interval	Do this
Warmup	Build from Level 1 to sweet spot over 10-15min with some bursts mixed in
1	Sweet spot 5min Sitting Sweet spot 5min Climbing Sweet spot 7min Mixmaster Level 1 5min
2	Sweet spot 5min Sitting Sweet spot 5min Climbing Sweet spot 7min Ladder Level 1 5min
3	Sweet spot 5min Sitting Sweet spot 5min Climbing Sweet spot 7min Super D
Cooldown	Level 1 10-15min

WEEK 11 - WORKOUT A

Interval	Do this
Warmup	Build from Level 1 to sweet spot over 10-15min with some bursts mixed in
1	Sprint 5sec Sweet spot 4:55 Sitting Sprint 5sec Sweet spot 4:55 Sitting Sprint 5sec Sweet spot 4:55 Sitting Level 1 5min
2	Sprint 5sec Sweet spot 4:55 Sitting Sprint 5sec Sweet spot 4:55 Sitting Sprint 5sec Sweet spot 4:55 Sitting Level 1 5min
3	Sprint 5sec Sweet spot 4:55 Sitting Sprint 5sec Sweet spot 4:55 Sitting Sprint 5sec Sweet spot 4:55 Sitting Level 1 5min
4	Sprint 5sec Sweet spot 4:55 Sitting Sprint 5sec Sweet spot 4:55 Sitting Sprint 5sec Sweet spot 4:55 Sitting
Cooldown	Level 1 10-15min

WEEK 11 - WORKOUT B

Interval	Do this
Warmup	Build from Level 1 to sweet spot over 10-15min with some bursts mixed in
1	Sweet spot 5min Sitting Sweet spot 5min Climbing Sweet spot 5min Mixmaster Level 1 5min
2	Sweet spot 5min Sitting Sweet spot 5min Climbing Sweet spot 5min Ladder Level 1 5min
3	Sweet spot 5min Sitting Sweet spot 5min Climbing Sweet spot 5min Super D Level 1 5min
4	Sweet spot 5min Sitting Sweet spot 5min Climbing Sweet spot 5min Super D
Cooldown	Level 1 10-15min

WEEK 12 - WORKOUT A

Interval	Do this
Warmup	Build from Level 1 to sweet spot over 10-15min with some bursts mixed in
1	Sprint 5sec Sweet spot 4:55 Sitting Sprint 5sec Sweet spot 4:55 Sitting Sprint 5sec Sweet spot 4:55 Sitting Sprint 5sec Sweet spot 4:55 Sitting Level 1 10min
2	Sprint 5sec Sweet spot 4:55 Sitting Sprint 5sec Sweet spot 4:55 Sitting Sprint 5sec Sweet spot 4:55 Sitting Sprint 5sec Sweet spot 4:55 Sitting Level 1 10min
3	Sprint 5sec Sweet spot 4:55 Sitting Sprint 5sec Sweet spot 4:55 Sitting Sprint 5sec Sweet spot 4:55 Sitting Sprint 5sec Sweet spot 4:55 Sitting
Cooldown	Level 1 10-15min

Printed in Germany
by Amazon Distribution
GmbH, Leipzig

WEEK 12 - WORKOUT B

Interval	Do this
Warmup	Build from Level 1 to sweet spot over 10-15min with some bursts mixed in
1	Sweet spot 5min Sitting Sweet spot 5min Climbing Sweet spot 5min Mixmaster Sweet spot 5min Ladder Level 1 10min
2	Sweet spot 5min Sitting Sweet spot 5min Climbing Sweet spot 5min Mixmaster Sweet spot 5min Super D Level 1 10min
3	Sweet spot 5min Sitting Sweet spot 5min Ladder Sweet spot 5min Mixmaster Sweet spot 5min Super D
Cooldown	Level 1 10-15min